THE EUCHARISTIC SACRIFICE

THE EUCHARISTIC SACRIFICE

By

DARWELL STONE, D.D.
PRINCIPAL OF PUSEY HOUSE, OXFORD

WITH APPENDED NOTES

Wipf & Stock
PUBLISHERS
Eugene, Oregon

Wipf and Stock Publishers
199 W 8th Ave, Suite 3
Eugene, OR 97401

The Eucharistic Sacrifice
By Stone, Darwell
ISBN: 1-59752-971-0
Publication date 9/20/2006
Previously published by The Morehouse Publishing Co., 1920

.

PREFACE

These six sermons were preached during Lent, 1919, at St. Paul's Church, Knightsbridge, and, with slight variations, at St. Barnabas's Church, Oxford. They are published in consequence of requests made by some who heard them. I have tried in the appended notes to remedy to some extent the scanty treatment necessarily imposed by the limits of sermons.

D. S.

January 5, 1920.

CONTENTS

vii

THE
EUCHARISTIC SACRIFICE

I

Sacrifice : Jewish, Pagan, and Christian

" Ye also as living stones are built up a spiritual house to be a holy priesthood, to offer up spiritual sacrifices acceptable to God through Jesus Christ." 1 St. Peter ii. 5.

IN considering the subject of sacrifice, Jewish, pagan, and Christian, we English people of the twentieth century, like English people of many past generations, are met by a difficulty at the outset. It is a difficulty which results from a difference between ourselves on the one side and Jews and pagans and early Christians alike on the other. To them the whole idea of sacrificial religion was familiar and ordinary ; to us for the most part it is unfamiliar and not at all ordinary except so far as we have recovered it by a somewhat difficult process of thought.

I

There are many resemblances between sacrificial ideas in the Old Testament and those in the New Testament, between those of pagans and those of early Christians ; but before I speak of these resemblances, I must say something about one obvious difference. For the Jews, the sacrificial idea was

embodied in the sacrifices of animals, of birds, of
flesh and blood, of meal, of wine ; and the sacrifices
were effected by a physical process ; they were
what we are accustomed to call carnal sacrifices.
So for the pagan, sacrifice meant the offering to
the deity of some human being, or animal, or thing,
most often by way of death or destruction. In
sharp contrast the Christian writers emphasize
that the sacrifices of the Christian religion are spiritual. They are " spiritual sacrifices " which St.
Peter says that the Christian Church is to offer
up.[1] It is a representative utterance of early Christian thought when St. Justin Martyr in the middle
of the second century writes, " We have received
that God needs not material offering from men."[2]
In some measure indeed this Christian view had
been anticipated in the Old Testament. Psalmist
and prophet had declared the inadequacy of sacrifices which were not accompanied by penitence
and righteousness, had represented the offerings
made by those whose hands were full of blood as an
offence to God ; and had made clear the supreme
part played in sacrifice by the dedication of the
will ; [3] but this great moral teaching left untouched
the place of sacrificed victims and material things
in the Jewish religion. The Christian argument
against sacrifices such as those of the Levitical

[1] 1 St. Peter ii. 5.

[2] St. Justin Martyr, *Apol.* 1. 10 : cf. 13 ; St. Irenaeus, *Adu.
Haer.* IV. xvii. ; Tertullian, *Ad Scap.* 2.

[3] See *e.g.* Ps. l. li. ; Isa. i. 10–17 ; Mic. vi. 6–8.

law was not that they were to be presented by the humble and the contrite but that they were not to be offered at all in Christian times.[1]

2

The repudiation of carnal sacrifices in the Christian religion marks an emphatic contrast between Christianity and Judaism, between Christianity and paganism. Besides the contrast there are some striking resemblances.

1. As a people the Jews were a priestly nation. To them were the divine words addressed, " If ye will obey My voice indeed, and keep My covenant, then ye shall be a peculiar treasure unto Me from among all peoples : for all the earth is mine : and ye shall be unto Me a kingdom of priests, and an holy nation."[2] To them as a nation was it spoken, " Ye shall be named the priests of the LORD : men shall call you the ministers of our God."[3] This very description is applied in the New Testament to the Christian Church. To Christians St. Peter wrote, " Ye are an elect race, a royal priesthood, a holy nation, a people for God's own possession."[4] Christians are described in the Book of the Revelation as " a kingdom and priests."[5] We Christians, says St. Justin Martyr again, " are the true high-priestly race of God."[6] The complete

[1] See note 1 on p. 57.　　[2] Exod. xix. 5, 6.
[3] Isa. lxi. 6.
[4] 1 St. Pet. ii. 9.　　[5] Rev. i. 6, v. 10.
[6] St. Justin Martyr, *Dial.* 116.

Christian, says Clement of Alexandria, " is truly the royal man, the holy priest of God."[1]

This priestly character of the whole nation of the Jews and of the whole society of the Christian Church, as it is depicted in the Old and New Testaments and in the writers of the early Church, includes three great marks. The Jewish nation, or the Christian society, has received the call and choice of God.[2] In consequence, it has a right of approach to God. And as a special way of approach, it has the right to offer sacrifice.[3] Thus, Jewish nation and Christian Church, despite their many differences, are alike in this : each is a sacrificial people with a special vocation from God which calls to sacrifice.

2. The priestly nation of the Jews needed a ministerial priesthood for the performance of its sacrificial rites. The offering made was the offering of the nation or of an individual within the nation ; but that it might be offered there was required the ministering priest who had been appointed by God and consecrated to his office. It was his work, to teach, to bless, to burn incense, to offer sacrifice. And so in the priestly society of the Christian Church there is need of the ministerial priests through whom the sacrificial functions of the society can be performed.[4]

3. In the Jewish sacrifices there were three main

[1] Clement of Alexandria, *Strom*. VII. vii. 36.
[2] See *e.g.* Exod. xix. 4, 5 ; 1 St. Pet. ii. 9.
[3] See *e.g.* Exod. xx. 24 ; 1 St. Pet. ii. 5.
[4] See note 2 on p. 59.

fundamental ideas.[1] First, the sacrifice was a gift from man to God. As a gift, it was an acknowledgment of God's power and supremacy, of the duty owed by the creature to the Creator. Secondly, it was a means of propitiation. The blood of the slain victim, itself the symbol of life, was offered to God as a means of pleading for forgiveness of sins. The constant meaning of the Levitical sacrifices is summed up by a sentence in the law. " The life of the flesh is in the blood : and I have given it to you upon the altar to make atonement for your lives : for it is the blood that maketh atonement by reason of the life."[2] Thirdly, the Jewish sacrifices were a means of communion between God and man. Man by reason of his nature possesses kinship to God. The truth " God created man in His own image, in the image of God created He him,"[3] lies behind all that is possible of human intercourse with the divine. On this kindred was built the fellowship which sacrifice made real. In sacrifice the worshippers took part in a sacred meal which they were regarded as sharing with Almighty God Himself. In it there was access to God.[4] In it the altar of sacrifice was also the table of the Lord.[5] In it the food was the bread of God.[6] As the worshipper brought his gift to God, God looked on

[1] See note 3 on p. 60.   [2] Lev. xvii. 11.   [3] Gen. i. 27.
[4] See e.g. Exod. xviii. 22 ; xxiv. 9–11 ; Deut. xii. 7.
[5] Ezek. xli. 22 ; xliv. 16 ; Mal. i. 7, 12.
[6] Lev. iii. 11, 16 ; xxi. 6, 8, 17, 21, 22 ; xxii. 25 ; Num. iii. 11, 16.

it and was well pleased ; and, still more, thereby God entered into a communion with him the closest then vouchsafed to man. This threefold aspect of sacrifice as gift, as propitiation, as communion, was not unknown in pagan religions. There too the sacred meal was closely connected with the sacrifice among most savage peoples and in a race so highly cultivated as the Greeks. This feature of paganism has its instruction for us as suggesting that such ideas on the one hand are attractive to human minds and on the other hand form part of that divine training for truth which has not been wholly lacking to any of the human race in God's care not to leave Himself without witness among any of the races of mankind. But for students of Christianity it is far less important than that Jewish practice and thought which were familiar to St. Paul, to the first apostles, and (we may reverently add) to the human mind of our Lord.

3

The sacrificial teaching of the New Testament reaches its height in the sacrifice of Christ Himself. Our Lord's earthly life, His death, His resurrection, His ascension, His heavenly life, are seen to include the aspects of sacrifice gathered from the Old Testament, gift, propitiation, communion. In Him are the dedication to God of a perfect human life, the means of divine forgiveness for man, the means of communion between man and God. He describes Himself as a sacrifice on our behalf. " The Son of man came not to be ministered unto, but to minister, and to give His life a ransom on behalf of many."[1] The blood of the new Covenant, which is His own blood, "is poured out on behalf of many unto remission of sins."[2] "The bread which I will give is My flesh on behalf of the life of the world."[3] "I am the good shepherd : the good shepherd layeth down His life on behalf of the sheep."[4] He, writes St. Paul, "was delivered up because of our trespasses, and was raised because of our justification."[5] He, says St. Peter, "in His own self bare our sins in His body upon the tree, that we, having died unto sins, might live unto righteousness : by whose stripes ye were healed."[6] In rich abundance the sacrificial phraseology of the Old Testament is applied to Him. He is the Lamb of God which taketh away the sin of the world.[7] He is our passover.[8] He is the propitiation for our sins.[9] He "gave Himself on our behalf an offering and a sacrifice to God of an odour of a sweet smell."[10] He made peace through the blood of His cross ;[11] and His blood cleanseth us from all sin.[12] In the Old Testament victim, the blood was the symbol of life, not of death. It was when the blood of the slain victim was poured out before God that the

[1] St. Matt. xx. 28 ; St. Mark x. 45.
[2] St. Matt. xxvi. 28 ; cf St. Luke xxii. 20.
[3] St. John vi. 51.   [4] St. John. x. 11.   [5] Rom. iv, 25
[6] 1 St. Pet. ii. 24.   [7] St. John i. 29.   [8] 1 Cor. v. 7.
[9] 1 St. John ii. 2 ; iv. 10.
[10] Eph. v. 2.   [11] Col. i. 20.   [12] 1 St. John i. 7.

crucial moment in the propitiation was reached.[1]
So in the sacrifice of Christ, He who all His human
life long had offered Himself in dedication to the
Father and the Father's will, on the cross gave that
life to the uttermost in the surrender of death, and
then as our high priest and our great victim presented Himself before the throne of the Father,
making His human blood, the symbol and the essence
of His whole human life, His abiding sacrifice on
our behalf. As priest and victim He fulfilled the
whole typical significance of the offering on the
Jewish Day of Atonement. His death, like the
death of the victim in the Levitical sacrifices, was a
stage in the great dedication, a stage which led on to
the abiding heavenly presentation, as the death in the
Levitical sacrifices led on to the pouring out of the
blood. In the Lord Himself is the central sacrificial
life of all the universe. There have been pictures
of it all the world over. The sufferings of the brute
creation, the cries of women and children, the agonies
of men, the dedication of will in life and in death,
the rites, sometimes touching, sometimes repulsive,
of heathen religions, in particular the ordered
system of the Levitical law, all these have in their
different ways pointed on to the sacrifice of the
cross, to the sacrifice presented in heaven ; and in
the light of Christ alone can their meaning ever be
seen. In Him the surrender of the will, the most
vital of all the elements of sacrifice, reached its
utmost height. He offers Himself. The offering

[1] See note **4** on p. 61.

is of His human life, perfect in its morality, stainless in its holiness, completely dedicated to the Father's will without stint or reserve. The offering is filled with all the power and glory of His Godhead, so that from His infinite being an infinite efficacy is derived. His life is the centre and the strength of all Christian life and worship. As He is, so is the Church ; as He is, so is the Christian ; in His offering He offers those who are His. Of all religions Christianity is the most characteristically sacrificial; for it takes its pattern and its nature from Him who is its Lord and its Life. So in the New Testament Christian life and worship are represented as sacrifice. St. Paul links with the assertion of that communion with God which results from Christians being the body of Christ the exhortation that they present their bodies " a living sacrifice, holy, acceptable unto God," their " reasonable service."[1] He describes himself as the " priest of Christ Jesus unto the Gentiles, ministering the sacrifice of the Gospel of God, that the oblation of the Gentiles might be made acceptable, being sanctified by the Holy Ghost."[2] In the Lord's mortal life there is a centre : it is His death on the cross. In His risen being there is a centre again : it is His presentation of Himself at the Father's throne. He

---

[1] Rom. xii. 1.

[2] Rom. xv. 16. On this verse see W. Sanday and A. C. Headlam, *in loco ;* and W. Sanday, *The Conception of Priesthood in the Early Church and in the Church of England*, pp. 89, 90.

is the great sacrifice, from whom all other sacrifice
has its power. If we shall find that the Eucharist
is the sacrifice of the Christian Church, we shall
find a truth which is in harmony with the whole
current of the Christian faith.

II

Our Lord's Resurrection and the Eucharist

" He hath granted unto us His precious and exceeding great promises ; that through these ye may become partakers of the divine nature." 2 St. Peter i. 4.

I SPOKE last of sacrifice. There were three features of sacrifice which were prominent in what I said. First, the central element in sacrifice is the dedication of the will. Secondly, the supreme sacrifice has been offered by our Lord Jesus Christ in His becoming incarnate, in His mortal life, in His death, in His resurrection and ascension, in His presentation of Himself at the Father's throne. Thirdly, the Christian religion, since its whole spirit is the spirit of Christ, is the most characteristically sacrificial of all religions.

I

My subject now is our Lord's resurrection and the sacramental system of the Church, in particular the Eucharist. In placing together the resurrection and the sacraments I do not wish to consider them as two separate subjects but in their relation to one another. By the resurrection I mean the bodily resurrection. The evidence for the resurrection of

11

our Lord's body is strong. The actual fact of the resurrection receives cumulative testimony from St. Paul's First Epistle to the Corinthians, from the Gospels, from the general background of the New Testament, from the effect on the minds and characters of the apostles, from the profound impression made on the theology and the system of the primitive Church. Yet to-day it is said by many, partly by those who do not believe in the fact but partly also by some who do so believe, that the bodily resurrection of our Lord has no spiritual significance, that all which is of spiritual value in the idea of the resurrection is secured by the continued spiritual existence of Christ, and that, however some ages may have rested on and been helped by belief in the bodily resurrection, it is in no sense a necessary part of the Christian faith. This notion has extended further the already widespread tendency to dig a deep gulf between our Lord's bodily resurrection and the Christian life and Sacraments ; and, while the Sacraments have been thought of as historically springing out of either our Lord's teaching and acts or the life and work of the Church, their close connexion with His own being has been minimized or ignored. The fact is that a right conception of the Sacraments depends on the preservation of their relation to our Lord's own Person, in His death, in His resurrection, in His ascended life. To understand them, we must remember and give adequate force to three facts. There is, first, the distinctive character of man through creation whereby he possesses personality which enables him to be in communion with God. There is, secondly, the Incarnation. In the Incarnation the relations between God and man obtain a new character. In this there is a new use of that which is material. In Christianity that which is material is not laid aside but is given fuller force than it had either in Judaism or in paganism. In the Incarnation God glorified matter by making it His own not simply by possession but also by personal union. Christ used His body as well as His soul as the means whereby to redeem us ; and the sufferings and dedication of His body were something more than the mere expression of His mind and spirit and will. And, thirdly, through the Sacraments there is actual union between Christians and our Lord's incarnate life embodied in the life of His body.

2

What then is the relation of the Sacraments to the resurrection of the Lord ? Between His death and the life of the Church were His resurrection and ascension and the outpouring of the Holy Ghost. There are two aspects of His resurrection presented in the New Testament. His risen body is regarded both by St. Paul and by the writers of the Gospels as being the same body as that which died on the cross and was buried in the tomb. But it is regarded also both by the apostle and by the evangelists as in a greatly changed condition, as spiritual instead of carnal, with new characteristics, with powers of transcending the ordinary laws of nature known to us. Not to dwell longer on this point, it is not for nothing that the evangelists tell us that in His risen body the Lord passed through the closed doors, moved from place to place in a moment of time, and presented a strange appearance even to those who knew Him well.[1]

St. Paul has much to say about the influence of Christ's body and about the importance and destiny of Christian bodies. He declares that by the operation of the one Spirit all Christians were baptized into one body,[2] that is, the one body of Christ, and that through Baptism they are the body of Christ and severally His members ;[3] he declares that the Eucharistic gift is a participation in the body and the blood of Christ.[4] Similarly, he speaks of the bodies of Christians in ways which suggest that the body is used in the economy of grace. Christians are hereafter to possess bodies which will be incorruptible and glorious, full of power and spiritual.[5] The inheritance which they rightly anticipate is the redemption of the body.[6] It is part of their destiny that the Lord Jesus Christ will transform the body now in a state of humiliation so as to be conformed to His body in the glorious being which it has possessed since His resurrection.[7] To what the New Testament thus teaches about the body of Christ Himself and the bodies of Christians, we may add its teaching

[1] See note 5 on p. 63.
[2] I Cor. xii. 13.   [3] I Cor. xii. 27.   [4] I Cor. x. 16.
[5] I Cor. xv. 42, 43. [6] Rom. viii. 23.   [7] Phil. iii. 21.

concerning the Holy Ghost. In the New Testament we are taught concerning the activities of the Holy Ghost on the risen body of Christ Himself at His ascension. Being exalted at the right hand of the Father He received from the Father the promised gift of the Holy Ghost.[1] We are taught also concerning the activities of the Holy Ghost on our own bodies. It is through the operation of the Holy Ghost that in Baptism, the gate of all other Sacraments, our bodies are made the means through which we receive spiritual grace.[2] Nor is this surprising when we remember the intimate union which exists between body and soul, and the influence of each upon the other. In our spiritual actions of faith and prayer we use our bodily brain as the instrument of spirit ; in all kinds of actions which are instinct with spiritual purposes the spirit uses the body ; the body is the vehicle of temptation to the spirit, and to the spirit bodily temptations are due. The nature of man is a unity, and one sphere of his being always has influence on the other sphere. In the Second Epistle of St. Peter it is said to be a result of the Incarnation that Christians are partakers of the divine nature.[3] Viewed in its context and in connexion with other teaching contained in the New Testament this statement shows that Christians actually receive the Holy Ghost, and through His operation are brought into actual union with the deity of Christ by means of His human nature, body and soul. To whatever

[1] Acts ii. 33.   [2] I Cor. xii. 13.   [3] 2 St. Pet. i. 4.

extent the body of Christ is of spiritual value to Christians in the present life, to that extent His bodily resurrection is of spiritual importance.

The use of outward means and the application of these through the agency of the body may be found in all the Christian Sacraments. In Baptism the application of water to the body is the means whereby body and soul are regenerate. In Confirmation the body is touched by the laying on of hands or the anointing with chrism ; and both body and soul are indwelt by God the Holy Ghost. In Penance words of Absolution are spoken by the body and are heard by the body in order that body and soul may be cleansed from sin. In Unction the oil is applied to the body for the work of healing both body and soul. In Holy Orders hands are laid on the body that thereby spiritual ministerial powers may be received. In Matrimony an earthly compact and rite so affect the whole relation of two bodies and souls that the whole of married life receives the specific blessing of Almighty God. This line of thought is the heart of the Catholic tradition about the Sacraments. The more it is realized, the more fully may the reasonableness and the coherence of the whole sacramental system be perceived. It runs through all the Sacraments. But it reaches its height in regard to the Eucharist. In the Eucharist the Holy Ghost acts by His divine power on the risen body of Christ in heaven and on the earthly elements which have been offered on the altar, and He transforms those elements into the body and blood of Christ. This divine action postulates the abiding existence of Christ's human body; it assumes the spiritual state, unhampered by ordinary laws, of the body of Christ, through His resurrection and ascension; it utilizes that union of body and soul which makes it possible for each to be the servant of the other in spiritual life. We may notice how in each part of the Church at the present time stress is laid on the work accomplished by the body of Christ through the body of the communicant. In the Eastern Liturgy of St. Chrysostom the priest prays at the moment of his Communion, "Let not the reception of Thy holy mysteries, O Lord, be to me for judgment or for condemnation but for healing of soul and body." In the Latin Mass of the West the priest says, "Let not the partaking of Thy body, O Lord Jesus Christ, which I though unworthy do presume to receive, turn to my judgment and condemnation, but through Thy loving-kindness let it be profitable to me for the protection and healing of mind and body." In the English Prayer Book we pray in the Prayer of Humble Access, "Grant us therefore, gracious Lord, so to eat the flesh of Thy dear Son Jesus Christ, and to drink His blood, that our sinful bodies made be made clean by His body and our souls washed through His most precious blood, and that we may evermore dwell in Him, and He in us;" and the words of administration are, "The body of our Lord Jesus Christ, which was given for thee, preserve thy body and soul unto everlast-

ing life."[1] Dwelling evermore in Christ, Christ
evermore dwelling in us, everlasting life: these are
accomplished in us in body and in soul; these are
results which spring out of the abiding life of the
risen body of Christ.

But the process is not mechanical. Whatever
our belief or our unbelief, whatever our love or our
failure to love, the body of Christ is in the Sacrament on the altar when the great words of consecration have been said, the body of Christ is given
to us in our Communion. But our moral and
spiritual benefit depends on the will with which we
offer, the will with which we receive. The Eucharist
is the supreme instance in the life of the Church,
as the earthly ministry of Christ was the supreme
instance in the world's history, of both good and
evil possibilities arising through that which itself is
good. Christ came in the Incarnation that men
might receive the forgiveness and blessing of God.
The perversity and sin of some turned His coming
to their condemnation. "If I had not come and
spoken unto them, they had not had sin: but now
they have no excuse for their sin."[2] It is not
otherwise in the Eucharist. The Lord is there
present to pardon and strengthen and bless. But
to receive His blessing, our good will must go out
to meet His. Now, as in the days of His mortal
life, an evil will may change His glorious gift into
a sentence of condemnation. From such a convic-

[1] See note 6 on p. 65.   [2] St. John xv. 22.

tion came the passionate prayers of the middle ages, " I pray that this Holy Communion may not bring guilt upon me to condemnation, but may intercede for me for my pardon and salvation." And so the Eucharistic blessing has its place in that great Christian theology which ever recognizes on the one side the gifts of God and on the other the awful powers of man's free will.

To realize the meaning and the value of the Eucharist, we need to keep strong hold on the truth of our Lord's resurrection. And we are not likely to know what the resurrection really means except as we view it in the light of the Sacraments and especially of the Eucharist.

III

The Eucharist as Sacrifice

" By which will we have been sanctified through the offering of the body of Jesus Christ once for all." HEBREWS x. 10.

I NOW have to deal with the subject of the Eucharist as sacrifice. In beginning to do so, let me recall some part of what I have said before. That which is central in sacrifice is the dedication of the will. In true sacrifice there is always the gift of self. That gift may sometimes be in life and may sometimes be through death. Death has been brought into sacrifice by sin where apart from sin it need not have been. If it has ever been difficult for us to realize sacrifice without death, that is because of the dominance of sin in a fallen world. Of all sacrifices the sacrifice of Christ is the centre. In Him is the complete fulfilment of all that has been incompletely done in the many offerings throughout the world. From His supreme sacrifice Christian life and Christian worship derive their nature. The more they are like Him, the more are they full of sacrifice. The Eucharist is at the heart of Christian life, and is the climax of earthly Christian worship. Let us consider how far it has such a sacrificial character as may fit it to fill this place.

I

Let us recall the events in the Upper Room at the
Last Supper.   Merely on the human side they are
of touching import.   One who has lived a holy
life of faithful service is giving " for the greatest
of ends the greatest of gifts,"[1]   He is giving Himself.
Through the Agony and the Trial, through the death
on the cross, He is to make the final surrender of
His human will.   He has gathered round Him His
closest friends that they may eat with Him for the
last time before He dies.   In the meal He gives them
a memorial of Him to keep his memory ever fresh.
Each word that He speaks, each act that He per-
forms, is instinct with the sacrifice of Himself.   Nor
is this sacrificial element found only in the Lord's
own dedication.   It must needs have been suggested
to the minds of the apostles by the time of His
action and by His words and deeds.   It was the
time of sacrifice, the season of keeping the Passover.
The very Supper in which they shared with Him was
either the Passover itself or some Passover com-
memoration.   The things which He used in the
new rite were to Jewish minds themselves sacrificial.
To us English people there is nothing particularly
sacrificial about bread and wine except so far as we
have learnt to connect them with the Eucharist.
To the Jew they were habitually associated with the
fine flour of the meal offering and the wine of the
drink-offering.   He used words which to them were

[1] W. Pater, *Marius the Epicurean*, ii. 155.

full of sacrificial meaning. The memorial was
before God as well as a reminder to man. His
blood of the covenant, the new covenant in His
blood, recalled the covenant made by sacrifice.
The term " poured out " in the words " This is
My blood of the covenant, which is poured out for
many unto remission of sins " was the very phrase
which described the climax in the sacrifice of the
Jews.[1] Thus the scene in the Upper Room at the
Last Supper was full of a deep sacrificial import for
those who had eyes to see and ears to hear.

We may turn from the time of the Institution
of the Sacrament to the teaching of St. Paul. Un-
like the first apostles St. Paul had not been present
at the Institution, but the knowledge of the events
which happened then was part of that Christian
faith which he received and taught to others.[2]
To him the Eucharist was so clearly sacrificial that
one of the fancies of an unbelieving criticism has
been that the doctrine of the Eucharistic sacrifice
was invented by him. Not only does he use about
it phrases which imply sacrifice ; according to him
it fills the place in the Christian system which was
filled by sacrifice in the religions both of Jews and
of pagans.[3]

Behind all else that is sacrificial in the New Testament is our Lord's description of the sacred food,

[1] See note 7 on p. 68.

[2] I Cor. xi. 23 : cf. xv. 3.

[3] I Cor. x. 16–21 ; xi. 23–26. In I Cor. v. 7, 8 the Eucharist is not primarily referred to, but can hardly have been
altogether out of mind.

" This is My body," " This is My blood." The consecrated Sacrament is the Lord Himself. That which is presented to the Father when the offering is made is the Lord's body, the Lord's blood, His very life.

2

From the earliest days of the Church it has been the ordinary habitual practice, adopted naturally as a matter of course, to speak of the Eucharist as sacrificial. It is described as a sacrifice, as an offering, as a victim, as a priestly work. The place of it is called an altar ; he who ministers in it is called a priest ; the office of those who minister is the office of priesthood.[1] No explanation of such phrases is given by the earliest writers. They fit in too well with the whole conception of Christian worship, with the whole idea of the Christian religion, to seem to need explanation. They come to men's minds naturally as the appropriate words ; and when we are using appropriate language about anything, we do not spend much time in explaining it. But in these early writers there are hints given which afford some degree of explanation. The Eucharist is the memorial made by the Church of Christ's passion and death. " The Eucharist," says one writer, " is the flesh of our Saviour Jesus Christ, which suffered for our sins."[2] " The bread of the Eucharist," says another, " which our Lord Jesus Christ commanded us to offer for a memorial

[1] See note 8 on p. 69.   [2] St. Ignatius, *Smyrn*. 6.

of the passion."[1] " The passion of the Lord,"
says a third, " is the sacrifice which we offer."[2]
Further, it is the memorial made by the Church of
Christ's resurrection, and of His incarnate life as
a whole. It " is the flesh of our Saviour Jesus
Christ," says one, which " not only suffered for
our sins " but which also " the Father of His good-
ness raised."[3] Christ's command to Christians,
says another, was that they should " offer it as a
memorial of His Incarnation."[4] Moreover, it is
the means of union with the present sacrificial offering of Christ in heaven. In the heavens, it is said,
we Christians have " a temple," " a tabernacle,"
" an altar," to which " our prayers and oblations
are directed."[5] The centre of Christian life and
worship is the perpetual pleading of the ascended
Lord at the Father's throne. The altar and the
sacrifice in heaven are not an altar of wood or
stone and a sacrifice of carnal things ; but altar
and sacrifice alike are the abiding offering of that
sacred Manhood which the Son of God took for the
salvation of His people in the Incarnation, the
blood of which He shed in His death. In the offering thus made by the Lord the holy dead and the living priestly society of the Church on earth have their
place and share. Into it are gathered all the

[1] St. Justin Martyr, *Dial.* 41.
[2] St. Cyprian, *Ep.* lxiii. 17.
[3] St. Ignatius, *Smyrn.* 6.
[4] St. Justin Martyr, *Dial.* 70.
[5] St. Irenaeus, *Adu. Haer.* IV. xviii. 6.

elements of the sacrificial life which Christians live, the sacrifices of praise and prayers, of pity and chastity, of righteousness and holiness. He who keeps the feast with Jesus is raised to be with Him in His heavenly work. "Those who follow Christ" "stand at the divine sacrifices" and "reach to the very altar of God, where is the Lord Jesus Christ Himself, the High Priest of good things to come."[1]

The Eucharist then is the Church's sacrifice. In it the Church presents to the Father as a sacrificial offering the life of the Lord. It is His Body, it is His blood, it is Himself. As the offering of Him, it is the offering of all that He has, of all that He is, of all that He has been, of all that He ever can be. It is of Him, and therefore in it we plead His passion and death. It is of Him, and therefore in it we plead His risen and ascended life. By His own gift we offer Him as a sacrifice to the Father, the sacrifice of the living One who died and is alive for evermore. With Him we are allowed to unite ourselves, and offer ourselves, our souls and bodies, with Him to the Father. And thus taking our part in the great offering, we are enabled to pray for our own needs and the needs of all the Church. Into the great stream of the sacrifice we pour the joys and griefs and desires of mankind. There are the sorrows of Christ's people, the troubles and perils of nations, the sorrowful sighing of prisoners, the miseries of

[1] Origen, *In Leu. Hom.* vi. 2 ; vii. 2, ix. 1, 3, 4, 5, 6, 9, 10 ; *In Jud. Hom.* vii. 2 ; *In Jer. Hom.* xviii. 13 (al. xix.).

widows and orphans and all that are desolate and
bereaved, the necessities of strangers and travellers,
the helplessness and sadness of the weak and sickly,
the weakness of the aged and of children, the trials
and aspirations of young men and maidens.[1]   With
the body of the Lord we offer all that is our own,
our praise and thanksgiving, our supplications for
ourselves and our intercessions for others, our
confessions of sin and our resolutions of amendment.
In words written by a writer of genius, " There are
little children there, and old men, and simple
labourers, and students in seminaries, priests pre-
paring for Mass, priests making their thanksgiving ;
there are innocent maidens, and there are penitent
sinners ; but out of these many minds rises one
eucharistic hymn, and the great Action is the measure and the scope of it."[2]

3

This then is the central thought of the Eucharistic
sacrifice.   In it the Church presents to God the
Father the merits of Christ, the life of Christ, the
death of Christ, the resurrection of Christ, Christ
Himself, in pleading for all manner of needs.   Round
the central thought there have gathered many
explanations and interpretations in different places
and at various times.   Some of them have had wide
influence in theological thought and devotional

[1] Cf. *Missale Romanum*, Orationes ante missam, feria
quinta.

[2] J. H. Newman, *Loss and Gain*, p. 329.

practice. Three instances may be noticed here.

Some of the liturgical writers of the middle ages, both in the East and in the West, have regarded the Eucharist as a great spiritual drama in which the life, death, resurrection, and ascension of Christ are enacted before God the Father in mystery, not as a mere memory, since the reality of His body and blood in the consecrated Sacrament makes the mystical drama find a centre in the actual presentation. On this view of the Eucharist as a spiritual drama the vestments of the priest had each of them their mystic significance. According to one interpretation, the amice depicted the veil by which the Lord was blindfolded, the alb the shining robe in which Herod sent Him back to Pilate, the girdle the scourges, the maniple the cords with which He was bound, the stole the rope with which He was tied to the column, the chasuble the scarlet cloak which the soldiers put upon Him in mockery. So too each part of the service was given its significance. The Introit represented the entrance of the Lord into the world in the Incarnation, the Epistle the preaching of the apostles, the Gospel the preaching of Christ Himself, the Offertory His oblation of Himself, the canon the scene in the Upper Room, the fraction of the consecrated Host the separation of His body from His soul in His death, the commixture of the fragment of the Host in the consecrated wine the reunion of body and soul in His resurrection, the Blessing His ascension.[1]

[1] See note 9 on p. 70.

Others have seen some element of destruction associated by them with sacrifice, whether in the fraction of the consecrated Host, or in the separate consecration of the two species, or in the consumption of the consecrated species, or in the condescension by which the glorified body of the Lord is in the Sacrament as if in a state of humiliation.[1]

Others again have laid their chief stress on the union of the sacrifice on earth with that which our Lord does in heaven.[2]

Such interpretations and explanations will appeal to different minds with a different force. To some, for instance, it will be of greater spiritual profit to associate the offering of the sacrifice chiefly with our Lord's passion ; to others an association with His heavenly offering will make a stronger appeal.

The thoughts of some will turn most readily to the Upper Room wherein the Lord looked forward to the cross ; the minds of others will most easily be concentrated on the " Lamb standing, as though it had been slain,"[2] in the high heaven.

For all of us, whatever value we may attach to this or that detail of interpretation, it is well to keep our thought firmly fixed on the central idea. In the Eucharistic sacrifice we plead before God the Father the body and blood of Christ, His human life, made present in our midst on the altar by the consecration.

[1] See note 10 on p. 71.   [2] See note 11 on p. 73.
[3] Rev. v. 6.

IV

The Presence of Christ in the Eucharist

" And as they were eating, He took bread, and when He had blessed, He brake it, and gave to them, and said, Take ye : this is My body. And He took a cup, and when He had given thanks, He gave to them : and they all drank of it. And He said unto them, This is My blood of the covenant, which is poured out on behalf of many." ST. MARK xiv. 22–24.

WE have already considered the central fact in the Eucharistic sacrifice. The Eucharist is the presentation of the body and blood, the human life, of our Lord to God the Father by the Church. This central fact depends upon another fact. The consecrated Sacrament is the body and blood of the Lord. He is present, and therefore we offer Him in sacrifice to the Father. Moreover, this sacred presence explains the gift of God to ourselves. The Lord is in His Sacrament, and therefore He is not only offered in sacrifice to the Father, He is also in our Communion bestowed upon us. Thus, both for the sacrifice to the Father and for the gift to Christians there is need of the truth that at the consecration the bread and the wine are made to be the body and blood of Christ.

I

Writing to the Corinthians some thirty years after the institution of the Sacrament St. Paul refers to it. The reference is incidental. As often in the New Testament, there is no detailed exposition of doctrine. The words are addressed to those who already have been taught the Christian faith. It is assumed that they know it. That which they know is referred to without explanation in order to illustrate points of moral conduct. There is a common ground of truth known to the writer and to the readers to which the writer can easily and confidently appeal to support his argument. So St. Paul adduces the belief about the Eucharist which the Corinthians already have received to support the position which he maintains. " The cup of blessing which we bless, is it not a partaking of the blood of Christ ? The bread which we break, is it not a partaking of the body of Christ ? "[1] The cup not only when received but also when blessed or consecrated before reception is of the blood of Christ ; the bread not only when received but also when broken before reception is the body of Christ. And again, " Whosoever shall eat the bread or drink the cup of the Lord unworthily, shall be guilty of the body and blood of the Lord."[2] He assumes that the body and blood of the Lord are there ; otherwise an unworthy receiver, whatever his guilt in other respects, could not rightly be described as being guilty of the body and blood.   And

[1] I Cor. x. 16.   [2] I Cor. xi. 27.

again, " He that eateth and drinketh, eateth and
drinketh judgment unto himself if he discern not
the body."[1] The judgment pronounced depends
on the presence of the body. In thus assuming the
truth which we have come to know as that of the
real presence of the body and blood of Christ in the
Sacrament, St. Paul refers to the teaching which
he had himself received from the Lord and which
he had delivered unto the Corinthians concerning
the institution of the Sacrament.[2] The records of the
institution which are preserved by the Evangelists
suggest exactly the same doctrine as that which is
assumed by St. Paul. According to those records
the Lord identified that which He held in His hand
and then gave to the apostles with His body.[3]
And in the Fourth Gospel a momentous scene in the
conflict with the Jews and in the training of the
apostles is described. The Lord speaks of Himself
as the Bread of life. He says further, " The bread
which I will give is My flesh, on behalf of the life of
the world."[4] And again, " Except ye eat the flesh
of the Son of man and drink His blood, ye have not
life in yourselves. He that eateth My flesh and
drinketh My blood hath eternal life."[5] And again,
" He that eateth My flesh and drinketh My blood
abideth in Me, and I in him."[6] It is a " hard saying "[7]
alike to opponents and to disciples. It is a teaching

---

[1] I Cor. xi. 29. [2] I Cor. xi. 23.
[3] St. Matt. xxvi. 26 ; St. Mark xiv. 22 ; St. Luke xxii. 19.
[4] St. John vi. 51. [5] St. John vi. 53, 54.
[6] St. John vi. 56. [7] St. John vi. 60.

which leads to conflict, to doubt, to desertion. To conflict : " the Jews therefore strove one with another, saying, How can this man give us His flesh to eat ? "[1] To doubt : " many " " of His disciples, when they heard this, said, This is a hard saying ; who can hear it ? "[2] To desertion : " many of His disciples went back, and walked no more with Him."[3] Yes, conflict, doubt, desertion. Yet the merciful Lord, who will not break the bruised reed or quench the smoking flax, cannot take back one word of the " hard saying." He is very truth ; and to the truth which He has spoken He must hold fast. What He does is to turn to the inner band of the faithful few, and sadly ask of them, " Would ye also go away ? "[4] And the sad question draws out from St. Peter the answer of belief, " Lord, to whom shall we go ? Thou hast the words of eternal life."[5] So that eyewitness of the Lord's ministry who wrote the Fourth Gospel, familiar as he must have been with the constant celebration of the holy Sacrament, describes the impression made on his mind by the teaching of the Lord. It is that the Lord faces and bears the hostility of opponents and the alienation of the half-hearted and even to question His friends rather than leave unborne the testimony that His flesh and blood are to be His gift of life. The studies of recent years have taught us to distinguish different strains in the

[1] St. John vi. 52.   [2] St. John vi. 60.   [3] St. John vi. 66.
[4] St. John vi. 67.   Compare W. Bright, *Morality in Doctrine*, p. 336.   [5] St. John vi. 68.

witness of the New Testament. Of those strains
the three chief and three of the most different are
the Epistles of St. Paul, the Synoptic Gospels,
and the Fourth Gospel. The three concur in their
testimony that the original belief of the Christian
Church, founded on our Lord's own teaching, identified the consecrated Sacrament with His body
and blood.

2

As is the teaching of the New Testament, so
also is the tradition of the Church. It is quite true
that, if we examine the whole mass of the evidence
afforded by the Christian writers of, let us say, the
first six centuries, we find in some places and at
some times and with some individuals a certain
amount of obscurity, a certain amount of hesitation,
a certain amount of inconsistency. The same is
true about many other matters of belief also. But
there is a great main stream of testimony concerning
Eucharistic belief which, viewed in detail or viewed
as a whole, is extraordinarily impressive. In that
main stream, not in a side current here or there ;
in the great body of Christian teaching, not in
a stray sentence here or there, is to be found the
real witness of the Christian Church. That witness
is summed up in a clear utterance from the first
half of the fourth century, " You will see the
Levites bringing the bread and the cup of wine, and
placing them on the Table. And so long as the
supplications and prayers are not yet made, the

bread and the cup are bare elements. But when the great and marvellous prayers are completed, then the bread becomes the body, and the cup the blood, of our Lord Jesus Christ."[1] They are the words of the greatest of the fathers, St. Athanasius. They express clearly and accurately the tradition of the early Church.[2]

3

Let us notice the harmony of this truth with other parts of the Christian faith.

1. It is in harmony, in the first place, with that aspect of the Incarnation whereby the Incarnation is God's answer to man's passionate longing for Him. The prayer ascribed to Moses was, " Show me Thy glory."[3] The desire of the worshipper in the Greek mysteries was for " personal communion with the divine life."[4] The aspirations of the Jew and of the most religious among the heathen were to find their satisfaction in the coming of God Most High to be Man on earth. And the hidden presence of God made Man in the holy Sacrament is that abiding outcome of the Incarnation wherein we are to rest until the vision of His glory is unveiled.

[1] St. Athanasius, *Serm. ad bapt.* quoted by Eutychius of Constantinople, *De Pasch. et de SS. Euch.* 8 (*Migne, Patr. Gr.* xxvi. 1325, lxxxvi. 2401).

[2] For a full treatment of the teaching of the early Church on this subject, see the first volume of the present writer's *A History of the Doctrine of the Holy Eucharist.*

[3] Exod. xxxiii. 18.

[4] E. Hatch, *The Influence of Greek Ideas and Usages upon the Christian Church,* p. 290. See also note 12 on p. 74.

2. Secondly, it is in harmony with the method whereby in the Incarnation material things are made the vehicles of spiritual gifts. God the Son Himself took human flesh and blood to be inseparably united with His divine Person. That material human nature was the means whereby He revealed Himself and the Father, the means wherein He redeemed the world. It is in harmony that through the ages of His mystical life in His body the Church He should make the material things of bread and wine the vehicles of His presence, the veils of Himself.

3. Thirdly, the character of the Lord's manhood was miraculous. Indeed His human life was real and complete. He had body, mind, soul, spirit, as really, as completely, as any of ourselves. His human experience was an experience as rich as can befall any of the sons of men. But as it is portrayed in the Gospels it is always miraculous also. His first possession of human life is through her who is the Virgin as well as the Mother. His ministry, while it is always human, is always also using powers which are greater than human. His resurrection and ascension are the fitting ending of what He does visibly on earth. The marvel of the Eucharist is appropriate to the whole course of the Lord's miraculous life.

4. Fourthly, the wonder of His life has a special feature in His resurrection. Through that resurrection His human body still exists. It exists transformed, made spiritual, so that what always

was the vehicle of spiritual gifts is now capable of being itself spiritually bestowed. As the Eucharistic presence follows naturally from the fact of the Incarnation, so also it gives expression to the nature of our Lord's resurrection.

5. Fifthly, the doctrine of the Eucharistic presence is in close harmony with that teaching of the New Testament concerning the body of Christ and the bodies of Christians on which we spent some time a fortnight ago. As we considered then, one great means of the working of the Lord is that whereby He acts through His body, and through their bodies Christians receive from Him.[1]

6. And, sixthly and lastly, the Eucharistic presence is in harmony with the operations of God the Holy Ghost in the covenanted sphere of the Church's life. The Lord's mortal human life from its first beginning in the Virgin's womb to the close of its mortality on the cross was empowered by the Holy Ghost. That strength of the Holy Ghost in Him did not cease with His death but abides for evermore. And as the Lord's own human life was full of the Holy Ghost, so from the first the life of the Church has been endued with the gifts of the Spirit. The Holy Ghost is indeed, as St. Ambrose phrases it, " where life is " ; [2] and He has His own special operations among Christian souls. In Baptism the supernatural cleansing and life and power which are bestowed are His. In Con-

---

[1] See pp. 13–18, above.
[2] St. Ambrose, *De Spir. S.* i. 172.

firmation His is the strength given for the battle against sin. In Ordination the ministers of Christ receive Him to enable them to perform their priestly office and work. In Penance the contrition in the souls of sinners and the reality of Absolution are alike His gift. It is congruous with all the rest that He works in the Eucharist. At the prayer of the Church He descends on priest, on people, and on the earthly elements of bread and wine. He by whose divine operation the Son of God became Man in the Virgin's womb, who sustained and empowered that same Son of God's earthly life, who from the Day of Pentecost until to-day has wrought mightily in the Christian Church, has here the greatest of His Christian activities, He transforms the bread, He transforms the wine, so that they are the very body and blood of the Lord.

'Tis said, 'tis done : and like as we believe
   That He, true God, became for us true Man ;
As, clinging to the cross, our souls receive
   The mysteries of His redemptive plan ;
As we confess, " He rose, and burst the tomb,
Went up on high, will come to speak the Doom ; '

So may we see the bright harmonious line
   Of all those marvels stretching on to this,
A kindred master-work of power divine,
   That yields a foretaste of our Country's bliss,
When pilgrim hearts discern from earthly food
The quickening essence of His flesh and blood.[1]

---

[1] W. Bright, *Monthly Packet*, October 1873, being the first two verses of the hymn of which the other verses beginning " And now, O Father, mindful of the love " are No.

267 in *Hymns Ancient and Modern*, new edition 1904, and No. 302 in *The English Hymnal*. The third verse, as given in the *Monthly Packet*, was originally " Wherefore we sinners, mindful of the love." See also Dr. Bright's *Hymns and other Poems*, second edition.

V

Theological Conclusions

"My flesh is true food, and My blood is true drink." S⊤·
JOHN vi. 55.

I HAVE laid stress on central aspects of Eucharistic truth. In the sacrifice to God, the Church
offers to God the Father the body and blood, the
human life, of God the Son. As the gift to man,
the bread and wine are made by consecration to be
the body and blood of Christ. Both sacrifice to
God and gift to man require that the consecrated
Sacrament itself is the Lord's body and blood. Let
us consider in view of this certain opinions concerning the Eucharist which have been widely prevalent
in England since the sixteenth century.

I

We may pass by without comment explicit denials
of the Eucharistic sacrifice. They are too far re-
moved from the whole system of theology which
we have been considering for it to be profitable
for us to spend time on them now. It is more
important to notice a line of thought very influential
in the sixteenth century, very prevalent since
then in the English Church, not without attraction

at the present time. It was the theory of Archbishop Cranmer in England, of John Calvin abroad ; it is found in the writings of very many of the English post-Reformation divines. According to this theory the Eucharist may be called a sacrifice. But it is only a sacrifice in such a sense as prayer and thanksgiving can be called sacrifices ; it is merely a mental remembrance of Christ's sacrifice on the Cross ; besides prayer and thanksgiving and this mental remembrance the offering to God is only that made of themselves by those who take part in the service. This teaching indeed contains elements of value. It recognizes some great truths. It allows for the sacrificial character of worship in general. It allows that the Eucharist is a means by which Christian worshippers are reminded of their Lord. It allows, further, that the Eucharist is a means by which those worshippers may offer themselves to God in dedication to His will to perform His work and to live as He commands. But it fails in one crucial point. It does not allow for the great central fact that in the Eucharist the Church offers to God the Father in sacrifice the Lord Christ Himself, His body, His blood, His human life, present in our midst on the earthly altar, as He ever lives at the altar which is on high. On its positive side it is true as far as it goes ; when compared with the great tradition of the Catholic Church it is seen to be inadequate ; when it passes into denial, it becomes untrue.[1]

[1] See note 13 on p. 75.

2

Concerning the presence of Christ in the Eucharist there are different levels which different forms of Protestant thought have reached. I will mention three such forms which are representative, and which taken together cover wide ground.

1. First, there is the opinion connected with the name of the Swiss Reformer Huldreich Zwingli. The elements of bread and wine, it is said, do not undergo any change at the consecration. Before consecration they are bread and wine; and after consecration they are nothing more. Nor are they the means of conveying any specific gift. The use of them in the service makes them to be the symbols, the figures, the images, of our Lord; it makes them nothing more. Illustrations employed by Zwingli himself in his writings on the subject have much significance. He compares, for instance, the Eucharistic bread and wine with the flowers in the wreath of a bride. These are selected from among other flowers. They are used for a particular purpose. They are given some special dignity which the flowers that are like them do not possess. But notwithstanding this selection and use and dignity they remain flowers, and they are nothing more. Just so, he argues, the bread and the wine in the Eucharist are selected from other bread and wine, they are used in a particular way, they have some special dignity from that use; but after consecration, as before it, they remain bread

D

and wine, and they are nothing more. Again
Zwingli compares the Eucharistic elements with
the gold of a marriage ring. It is used as other
gold is not used. It may serve, and it ought to
serve, to remind the wife who wears it of her absent
husband. But it remains gold and it is nothing
more. So the Eucharistic bread and wine may
remind, and ought to remind, the Christian who
receives them of his absent Lord ; in themselves
they undergo no change. In another illustration
Zwingli compares the Eucharistic elements to the
signet ring of a king. The material of which the
ring is made is not altered as it receives its shape
and its purpose. Yet the use of it gives to that
material an excellence which otherwise it would
not possess. So the Eucharistic bread and wine
are not altered, though they have an excellence
which other bread and wine have not. Zwingli's
illustration from the signet ring suggests rather more
concerning the Eucharist than is suggested by the
other two illustrations. For a signet ring, if used as
a sign of authority or to seal a document, may
be the means of effecting something which a wedding
ring or a flower in a bridal wreath could not effect.[1]

2. Another form of Protestant opinion concerning
the Eucharist is that known as Virtualism. It has
been given this name because of the teaching that
those who faithfully receive the Sacrament receive
the virtue of Christ's body, although the Sacrament
itself is nothing more than bread and wine. Vir-

[1] See note 14 on p. 76.

tualism was the opinion eventually held by Archbishop Cranmer and advocated by him in the year 1550 and following years. It has been the view of many in the English Church.[1]

3. A third form of Protestant opinion has the name of Receptionism. Those who hold it maintain that, though the consecrated bread and wine remain bread and wine and are nothing more, yet faithful communicants at the time of receiving the Sacrament receive also the body and blood of Christ. This was the opinion of Bucer and Calvin in the sixteenth century ; it was defended by many of the post-Reformation English divines. The tendency of it has been to pass into Virtualism.[2]

Each of these three representative opinions has some spiritual value. In the order in which I have mentioned them, that value ascends and increases. To receive the body and blood of Christ, even though the Sacrament is not that body and blood, is more than to receive the virtue of the body and blood without the body and blood themselves. To receive the virtue of the body and blood is more than to receive merely a figure and emblem of the body and blood. Even the bare figure, the mere memory, has the value of a sign to assist the Christian in remembering his Lord. But any one of these opinions fails to do justice to the teaching of the New Testament and of the Church ; any one of them is inadequate for preserving that central fact which, as we have seen, is a vital part of the

[1] See note 15 on p. 77.　　[2] See note 16 on p. 78.

true doctrine concerning the Eucharistic sacrifice and the Eucharistic presence, the fact that the consecrated bread and wine are the body and blood of Christ.

3

Opinions then like those of Zwingli and of Cranmer and of Calvin must be set aside if the central truth of the Eucharist is to be maintained. On the other hand, there are many differences of explanation and interpretation which leave that central truth unimpaired. A fortnight ago we noticed that this was the case in regard to the Eucharistic sacrifice; to-day let us observe this in regard to the Eucharistic presence.

1. There has been much difference within the Church as to the question who is rightly described as the Agent, the Worker, in the consecration. The characteristic view in the West has been that the principal Agent in the work of consecration is our Lord Himself, that the priest acts as His representative in His name, and that consequently the priest speaks the words of consecration in the power and Person of Christ. Also in the West it has often been taught, sometimes together with the teaching that our Lord is the principal Agent, that the priest in consecrating is the representative of the Church, and speaks in the name of the Church. The characteristic Eastern view is different, namely, that the consecration is effected by God the Holy Ghost in response to the prayer of the priest and the Church.

Now the truth probably is in the combination of these two aspects of it ; but not to enter upon this question, even if either of them were pushed to the exclusion of the other the central fact that the consecrated Sacrament is the body and blood of Christ would remain.[1]

2. There is another difference as to the means and the moment of consecration. It is the characteristic Western view that the consecration is effected by the recital of our Lord's words used at the institution of the Sacrament, This is My body, This is My blood. This is the explanation adopted both by the Church of England and by the Church of Rome. The characteristic Eastern view is that the consecration is effected by the invocation of the Holy Ghost, the prayer addressed to God the Father that He will send the Holy Ghost upon the elements to make them the body and blood of His Son. The difference here is by no means unimportant; but even if it is pushed to its most acute form, on either explanation the central truth remains.[2]

3. There has been difference, leading often to bitter controversy, as to the method of the presence of Christ in relation to the elements. Since the fourth or fifth century there have been two distinct lines of thought within the Church on this matter. One of these lines of thought has been in the direction of the doctrine known as Transubstantiation. The other has been against it. The tendency of

[1] See note 17 on p. 79.
[2] See note 18 on p. 80.

the first has been to lay stress on the greatness of
the change, the completeness of the transformation,
effected by the consecration. As definitions grew
more precise, it led to the explicit assertion that
after the consecration the substance or essential
reality of the bread and wine no longer exists, so
that, while the accidents or qualities which the senses
can discern still remain, there is in the Sacrament
after consecration only one substance, the substance
of the body and blood of Christ. The tendency of
the other line of thought has been to emphasize
the parallel of the Incarnation. As in the incarnate
Lord, it is said, there is the true nature, the essential
being, of God, and also the true nature, the essential
being, of Man, so in the consecrated Sacrament
there is the essential reality of the body and blood
of Christ, and also the essential reality of the bread
and wine.[1] Here again there are important issues
involved in the difference ; but they do not touch
what is of main consequence to the Christian.
That which matters to the Christian is what is
present in the Sacrament, not what is absent. If
the Christian can say, Here in the consecrated
Sacrament, hidden beneath the veil of the outward
part, is in all truth and reality the body and blood of
my Lord, it does not concern him very much whether
the essential reality of the bread and wine are
still there or are not. He can concentrate his
thought on the very presence of the living Lord ;

[1] See note **19** on p. 82.

he need not distract his attention by questioning what else is there.

I have mentioned three differences of opinion among those who are agreed that at consecration the bread and wine are made to be the body and blood of Christ. About them, and particularly about the last, there is a vast literature. They are the kinds of questions about which men's minds are likely to be divided until the end of time. In the right place they may need discussion. For most of us it is our wisdom to fix our thought chiefly on what I have called again and again the central truth, the fact of the real presence on the altar in the Sacrament of our Lord and God.

VI

Practical and Devotional Conclusions

"I beseech you therefore, brethren, by the mercies of God, to present your bodies a living sacrifice, holy, acceptable to God, which is your reasonable service." ROMANS xii. 1.

WE have considered different aspects of the Eucharist. It has all the marks of sacrifice. In it we plead before God the Father the propitiation accomplished by God the Son ; in it we make our gift to God of the material elements, and receive them back from Him transformed into the body and blood of Christ ; in it we dedicate ourselves to God's service in union with the dedication of Christ ; in it we find the closest communion with God ; in it we offer to the Father the human life, the death, the resurrection, the ascension, of His Son ; in it we receive from Him that same human life of the Son to be the food of our souls. As sacrifice, as Communion, there is the central truth that the consecrated Sacrament is the body and blood of the Lord.

There are certain practical conclusions which follow from this central truth.

I

The first of these practical conclusions concerns the place which the Eucharist fills in Christian worship and in Christian life. If we are really taking home to our hearts the theological truth, we cannot leave it to be only an intellectual apprehension. It must do something to shape our prayer, and it must do something to shape our lives. In so far as it is realized in our whole being, it will make imperious demands. The Eucharist, then, not only because it is the one service directly instituted by our Lord but also because of what it is in itself, will claim the chief place in our worship. It will do this in more ways than one. It is the service of primary obligation. Those who recognize what it is will not except through grave necessity allow a Sunday or other high festival to pass without their taking some part in it. Those who recognize what it is will desire that as opportunity is theirs it may hallow each day of their lives. It is the chief moment of prayer, into which are gathered hopes and fears, yearnings and entreaties, intercessions for others, supplications for ourselves. It is the service of principal dignity. The circumstances and outward fashion in which it is celebrated will be designed to show something of its meaning, something of its beauty, something of its grandeur. It will be approached with due preparation of body and soul. Those who draw near to receive the body of the Lord will desire for their own bodies all possible freshness, will desire to make this sacred food the first food of the day of Communion, will desire that their souls be cleansed from all defilements of sin. From Eucharistic prayer and Communion Christians go forth to the battle and stress or the monotony and weariness of daily life. In the sanctuary they find their joy and their strength. From the sanctuary they carry with them the great gift which they have received. Day by day they strive to live a Eucharistic life which ever looks back to the Communion last received and forward to that which is to come. From the altar they take with them the Lord Himself to be their Companion in pain and in delight, in effort and in rest, in the bright hours of youth, in the steadier glow of middle life, in the waiting of old age. He is still what He has ever been, Example, Redeemer, Friend, our Lord and God. He sets the standard what to do and what to be. He delivers in temptation and upholds from sin. He enlightens with His own gladness those who are faithful to the living Presence which He has bestowed on them.

2

The attitude of the Christian towards his Saviour received in Communion has thus a permanent character. But it will be affected by, and will in turn affect, the movement of his soul towards the Lord at the moment of the consecration in the Mass. We worship God indeed through all the universe. We speak to Him in our houses, in the streets, in the fields, in the train, on the sea. Always and everywhere He is our God, and we worship Him. But our Lord and Saviour in the degrees of His divine presence, in the manifestation of His human nature, is closer and nearer through the supreme way of His covenanted gifts as on the altar He vouchsafes to make Himself known. And therefore with a special adoration we bow before Him when the consecration makes the earthly elements to be the veils of His being, and while the consecrated Sacrament remains in our midst. All that we can offer as the tribute of love in the form of worship we pour out in the Sacrament to our Friend and our God.

Prostrate I adore Thee, Deity unseen,
Who Thy glory hidest 'neath these shadows mean.
Lo, to Thee surrendered my whole heart is bowed,
Tranced as it beholds Thee, shrined within the cloud.
Sight and touch and taste are all in Thee deceived,
'Tis the hearing only safely is believed.
I believe whate'er the Son of God hath told,
What the Truth hath spoken, that for truth I hold.
'Twas the Godhead only on the Cross was veiled,
Here the Manhood also is from sight concealed.
Both alike believing, Thee one Christ I own,
Suing, like the robber, at Thy mercy's throne.
Thy dread wounds, like Thomas, though I cannot see,
His be my confession, Lord and God, of Thee.
Lord, my faith unfeignéd evermore increase,
Give me hope unfading, love that cannot cease.
Oh, memorial wondrous of the Lord's own death,
Living Bread, that givest all His creatures breath,
Grant my spirit ever by Thy life may live,
To my taste Thy sweetness never-failing give,
Pelican most tender, Thine own children's food,

Cleanse my heart's uncleanness with Thy precious blood.
Lo, one drop, dear Jesu, all the world could save,
From sin's foul pollution all creation lave.
Jesu, whom, now veiléd, I by faith descry,
What my soul doth thirst for, do not, Lord, deny,
That Thy face unveiléd I at last may see,
With the blissful vision blest, my God, of Thee.[1]

3

The Church's belief about the Eucharist has led
to a strong sense of the responsibility which rests
on those who are the custodians of the Sacrament.
The first Oecumenical Council, when legislating
concerning the dying, spoke of the Eucharist as
" the last and most necessary Viaticum."[2] The
earliest description of the Celebration of the Eucharist outside the New Testament records that the
Sacrament was carried from the place of worship
to those who were absent from the service.[3] Practical experience has shown that, if adequate provision
is to be made for the sick and dying, and also for
some who are neither sick nor dying, the Sacrament
must be continuously reserved in church. When
it is so reserved, those who realize what the Sacrament is will not be content that it should be deprived
of its due honour. They will look for a seemly and
dignified method of reservation. They will look
for a fitting place. They will claim that when they

[1] St. Thomas Aquinas, *Opuscula*, xvii. (al. lvii.), as translated by E. B. Pusey in his edition of J. M. Horst's *Paradise
for the Christian Soul*, p. 405.

[2] Council of Nicaea (A.D. 325), can. 13. See note **20** on
p. 83.

[3] St. Justin Martyr, *Apol.* i. 65, 67.

are in the presence of the Sacrament they may worship and praise and pray in their realization that
He who is hidden there is their Lord and God.
They will recognize indeed that much in the methods
of reservation must be determined by authority,
they will acknowledge in particular that services
of devotion gathered round the reserved Sacrament must, like all other acts of public worship,
be under the control of the bishop of the diocese.
But for themselves they know, with a certainty
which springs from the security of their belief,
that they must worship our Lord where the
Sacrament is reserved with that fulness of adoration
which they feel and express towards Him in the
Mass. It is again the same great central truth.
He who is in the Sacrament is the Son of Mary and
the Son of God, Himself the most glorious of all
the sons of men, Himself true and eternal God,
to whom is due the uttermost of all that we can
give.[1]

4

A leading feature in the lives of the earliest Christians was their gladness. You may see it in the
record of the first Church in the Acts of the Apostles.
You may observe it constantly as the dominant
tone of the Epistles. It passes outside the New
Testament and is perhaps the most characteristic
mark of the Church of the second and third centuries

[1] For a fuller treatment of Reservation, see the present
writer's *The Reserved Sacrament.*

in the midst of suffering and persecution and toil. It was not unconnected with the Eucharist. We read in the Acts, " And day by day, continuing steadfastly with one accord in the temple, and breaking bread," that is, celebrating the Eucharist, " at home, they did take their food with gladness and singleness of heart, praising God."[1]   The very name Eucharist means thanksgiving. " The Eucharist of those early days," says an acute and sympathetic writer not himself wholly committed to Christian belief, referring to the second century, " was even more completely than at any later or happier time, an act of thanksgiving," and he speaks of " the sustained gladness of the rite," and pictures the educated pagan who has chanced to be present at it as going away wondering whether it is this " strange scene " of worship which has " made the way of " his Christian friend " so pleasant through the world."[2]   This gladness of the early Church gathered round the Sacrament. It had its force in two great convictions. The first of them was the sense of deliverance. Christ had set Christians free ; and the freedom included the power to conquer sin and live in holiness. And the second was the sense of personal communion with God. These two convictions underlie all the splendid defiance of the early Church. Christians may be persecuted, they may seem to be overcome, some of them through their faithlessness may even fall into sin ;

[1] Acts ii. 46, 47.
[2] W. Pater, *Marius the Epicurean*, ii. 156, 157.

but still they have that which it is worth the surrender of everything else to possess, they have,
as no others have, the power of righteousness and of
union with God. So with a great confidence these
early writers make their appeal, If you want to
know that sin can be conquered, you may see it
in us. During the last half century or so a great
deal of the bright gladness which the English
Church was in danger of losing has been brought
back to the Sacrament. Such a restoration is good.
But it suggests to us some solemn questions. Are
we of the English Church as a body, as a society,
giving due effect to our unseen inheritance, our
Christian union with God through the Sacraments
of His grace ? Do we tend at all to lean too much
on earthly things, on the arm of flesh, on outward
resources, on system and organization ? Are we as
capable as the early Church of the bold challenge,
You can see that Christianity is true by the lives
of Christians ? Can we say with all the confidence
which they possessed, We Christians hold the solu-
tion of the world's riddles, We Christians have the
remedy for all the world's pain and sin, It is
because of our prayers and lives that the world is
not wholly corrupt ?[1] Whatever the right answer
to these questions concerning the English Church
as a society may be, there is a consideration which
presses home on each one of us individually. Every
time that we make our Communion, every time
that we are present at the offering of the sacrifice,

[1] See note 21 on p. 84.

every time that we visit the reserved Sacrament, we are met by a challenge. It is the challenge of our Lord, who recalls our minds to what He is and what He has done. There is before us the memorial which is at once the reminder to ourselves and the presentation to God the Father, the memorial of the human life of God the Son. We see the stainlessness of His purity, the completeness of His holiness, the greatness of His self-sacrifice. By our Communion we claim that, as we plead all this before the Father, so also we receive it into ourselves. We are the Christ-bearers,[1] filled with the power of His life, able, if only we will use that power, to reproduce its splendour. And the supreme triumph of the Christ of the Eucharist is as He conforms our lives to His.

[1] See note 22 on p. 86.

NOTE 1. See p. 3

EARLY CHRISTIAN TEACHING CONCERNING JEWISH SACRIFICES

Two ways of regarding the Jewish sacrifices are found in early Christian writers.

1. Sometimes it is maintained that even in pre-Christian times the Jews had been mistaken in performing the sacrifices of the Jewish law, and that the injunctions understood to command these ought always to have been regarded as metaphorical. Thus, the commands for sacrifices, circumcision, the temple, distinctions in food ought always to have been understood spiritually only. The most remarkable instance of this line of thought is *The Epistle of Barnabas*, probably written at Alexandria between A.D. 70 and A.D. 79, not by the companion of St. Paul but by another writer of the same name. Other possible instances are the *Apology* of Aristides (written at Athens about A.D. 140) and the *Epistle to Diognetus* (probably written at Athens about A.D. 150).

2. The more usual view was that the Jewish sacrifices were intended to be performed but were instituted as a concession to the hardness of heart which characterized the Jews, and belonged to a past dispensation. See *e.g.* St. Justin Martyr, *Dialogue with Trypho*, 22 (probably written at Rome about A.D. 155); Tertullian, *Against Marcion*, ii. 18, 22 (Africa, about A.D. 205). Very representative later expressions of this view are in St. Gregory of Nazianzus, *Orations*, xxxi. 25 (Constantinople, about A.D. 380); St. Cyril of Alexandria, *Against*

E

Julian, iv. (Aubert, vi. (2). 126) (Alexandria, about A.D. 433) ; St. Gregory the Great, *Epistles*, xi. 76 (also in Bede, *Ecclesiastical History*, i. 30) (Rome, A.D. 601).

It was agreed by all that such sacrifices as the Jews had used ought not to be offered by Christians.

NOTE 2. See p. 4

MINISTERIAL PRIESTHOOD

The nature of the ministerial priesthood in the Church of Christ is discussed at length in R. C. Moberly, *Ministerial Priesthood*. See also the present writer's *The Christian Church*, pp. 233–324.

In the Old Testament sacrifice originally apparently was independent of an official priesthood or an appointed place : see *e.g.* Gen. iv. 3–5 ; viii. 20, 21 ; xxxi. 54 ; xlvi. 1 ; Jud. vi. 19–32 ; xiii. 19–21 ; Job i. 5 ; in the fully developed system sacrifice was limited to the central sanctuary, and a priest was needed to manipulate the blood of the victim slain by the person offering the sacrifice (Lev. i. 5) or a Levite (Ezek. xliv. 11) : see *e.g.* Lev. i.—v. The ministerial priests thus needed were appointed by God and consecrated to their office : see Exod. xxviii. 1—xxix. 35. Their work besides sacrifice included teaching (see *e.g.* 2 Chron. xv. 3 ; cf. Deut. xvii. 9–13), burning incense (see *e.g.* 1 Chron. xxiii. 13 : cf. Deut. xxxiii. 10 ; 1 Sam. ii. 28), and blessing the people (see 1 Chron. xxiii. 13 ; Num. vi. 22–27 : cf. Deut. x. 8 ; xxi. 5).

NOTE 8. See p. 5

SACRIFICE AS GIFT AND PROPITIATION AND COMMUNION

For the conception of sacrifice as a gift from man to God see *e.g.* Gen. iv. 3–5 ; Jud. vi. 18–21, xiii. 15–19 ; 1 Sam. ii. 17, 29, xxvi. 19 ; 1 Kings iii. 4, viii. 64 ; Exod. xxix. 38–42 ; Num. xvi. 15, xxviii. 3–15. For the conception of propitiation see *e.g.* Exod. xii. 7, 13, xxiv. 5–8, xxix. 36, 37, xxx. 10 ; Lev. i. 4, iv. 20, 26, 31, 35, v. 10, 13, 16, 18, vi. 7, xiv. 20, xvi. 24, xvii. 11. As to the conception of communion, there was the general connexion of sacrifice with a meal as a symbol of fellowship (see *e.g.* Gen. xxxi. 54 ; Exod. xii. 8–11 ; Lev. vii. 11–34 ; 1 Sam. i. 4–9, ix. 12, 13) ; the place of sacrifice was regarded as the place of approach to God (see *e.g.* Exod. xxix. 42–46) ; the sacrifice was a means of approach to God (see *e.g.* Exod. xviii. 12, xxiv. 9–11 ; Deut. xii. 7 ; Prov. ix. 1–5) ; the altar was the table of God (Ezek. xli. 22, xliv. 16 ; Mal. i. 7, 12) ; and the sacrifice was the bread of God (Lev. iii. 11, 16, xxi. 6, 8, 17, 21, 22, xxii. 25 ; Num. xxviii. 2). If a division is made into five kinds of sacrifice, (1) the burnt offering, (2) the meal offering, (3) the peace offering, (4) the sin offering, (5) the guilt offering (see Lev. i.—v.), the conception of gift may be seen in all, the conception of propitiation in the burnt and sin and guilt offerings, the conception of communion in the eating of the peace offering by the maker of the offering and others and in the eating of parts of the meal and sin and guilt offerings by the priests.

NOTE 4. See p. 8

See p. 8

BLOOD IN THE OLD AND NEW TESTAMENTS

For the ideas connected with blood in the Old and New Testaments see B. F. Westcott, *The Epistles of St. John*, pp. 34–37.

For the application of the blood in the Old Testament sacrifices see B. F. Westcott, *The Epistle to the Hebrews*, p. 291, " The blood was applied by the priests only, and in four different ways.

" i. It was 'sprinkled' (*zarak, to asperse*), *i.e.* probably it was all thrown about from the bowl directly or by the hand from the bowl ' on the altar [of burnt-offering] round about ': Lev. i. 5, iii. 2, vii. 2, etc. This was done in the case of burnt, peace, and guilt offerings.

" ii. It was 'applied' (*nathan, to give*) to the horns of the altar of burnt offering, and the remainder poured out at the base of the altar : Lev. iv. 30. This was done in the case of a sin offering for ' one of the common people.'

" iii. It was carried into the holy place, and some of it was applied to the horns of the altar of incense and sprinkled (*hizzah*) with the finger upon the veil seven times : the remainder was poured out at the base of the altar of burnt offering : Lev. iv. 6, 17, 18. This was done in the case of a sin offering for a priest or for the congregation.

" iv. It was carried into the holy of holies and sprinkled with the finger ' upon the mercy-seat, and before the mercy-seat seven times ': afterwards it was applied to the horns of the altar of burnt offering, and sprinkled upon it with the finger seven times : Lev. xvi. 14, 15, 18, 19. [Nothing is said of the disposition of the remain-

der of the blood.]   This was done on the Day of Atonement."

See also the articles on "Sacrifice in the Old Testament " by G. H. Box and " Sacrifice in the New Testament " by F. E. Brightman in *Murray's Illustrated
Bible Dictionary* (edited by W. C. Piercy), pp. 760–
769.

NOTE 5. See p. 14

OUR LORD'S RISEN BODY

In the New Testament there are two aspects of our Lord's resurrection.

1. His risen body was the same body which was buried in the tomb since there was an actual bodily resurrection from the tomb. This is indicated in the teaching of St. Paul, in the Synoptic Gospels, and in the Fourth Gospel. In St. Paul the actual bodily resurrection is implied in 1 Cor. xv. 3, 4 by (1) the word ἐγήγερται, *has been raised*, (2) the way in which the death and burial and resurrection are spoken of as parallel facts, (3) the emphasis on " the third day," which would be meaningless if all that was meant was a continuance of spiritual existence. In the Synoptic Gospels it is shown by (1) the description of the empty tomb and the whole narratives in St. Matt. xxviii. 1–6, 11–15 ; St. Mark xvi. 1–11 ; St. Luke xxiv. 1–35 ; (2) the emphasis on the " third day " in the prophecies of the Passion ; see St. Matt. xvi. 21, xvii. 23, xx. 19 ; St. Mark viii. 31, ix. 31, x. 34 ; St.Luke ix. 22, xviii. 33 (not in ix. 44) : cf. St. Matt. xii. 40, xxvii. 63, 64 ; St. Luke xxiv. 6, 7, 21, 46.

2. There was a change in the body so as to make it a spiritual body. This aspect, like the first, is found in St. Paul, the Synoptic Gospels, and the Fourth Gospel. In Rom. vi. 9, 10 St. Paul suggests an essential difference between Christ's life before the resurrection and His life after the resurrection since in the life after the resurrection He is inherently incapable of dying. In 1 Cor. xv. 35–54 St. Paul evidently views the risen bodies of Chris-

tians as being like the risen body of Christ, and describes these as "raised in incorruption," "in glory," "in power," "spiritual." In the Synoptic Gospels and in the Fourth Gospel there are indications of the spiritual character of our Lord's risen body in St. Matt. xxviii. 2 ; St. Mark xvi. 12 ; St. Luke xxiv. 16, 31 ; St. John xx. 14, 15, 19, 26, xxi. 4.

It is probably right to distinguish our Lord's walking on the sea in His pre-resurrection body as an exercise of His miraculous power from the acts in which His risen body exercised its new powers as a spiritual body. But there appears to have been an anticipation of the spiritual powers of His risen life in the Transfiguration and in the gift of His body and blood to the apostles at the Last Supper.

On the whole subject see B. F. Westcott, *The Revelation of the Risen Lord*, pp. 7–10. See also an excursus " On the condition of our Lord's human body " in H. N. Oxenham, *The Catholic Doctrine of the Atonement*, pp. 358–362.

NOTE 6.   See p. 18

THE EUCHARISTIC GIFT TO THE BODY OF THE COMMUNICANT

The body of the communicant has not always been mentioned in the words of administration.   In the early Church Order as given in the *Verona fragment* (E. Hauler, pp. 112, 113) the words were " Heavenly bread in Christ Jesus," " In God the Father Almighty and the Lord Jesus Christ and the Holy Ghost and the Holy Church," as in the Ethiopic text of the so-called " Egyptian Church Order," " This is heavenly bread, the body of our Lord Christ," " This is the blood of our Lord Jesus Christ " (G. Horner, *The Statutes of the Apostles*, p. 156 : cf. 200), and as in the *Canons of Hippolytus*, " This is the body of Christ," " This is the blood of Christ " (*Canons of Hippolytus*, 146, 147).   Words used in the sixth century were " The body of our Lord Jesus Christ preserve thy soul " (see John the Deacon, *S. Gregorii Papae Vita*, ii. 41).   An English pre-Reformation use is given as " The body of our Lord Jesus Christ preserve thy body and thy soul unto eternal life " in the *York Manual* (p. 51* in vol. lxiii. of the Surtees Society's publications).   In the English Order of Communion of 1548 the words were " The body of our Lord Jesus Christ which was given for thee preserve thy body unto everlasting life," " The blood of our Lord Jesus Christ which was shed for thee preserve thy soul to everlasting life." In the Prayer Book of 1549 " thy body and soul " was said at the administration of both species.   In the Church of Rome the words still are " The body of our Lord Jesus Christ preserve thy soul unto eternal life "

(*Rituale Romanum*).   The Eastern words do not mention either body or soul : they are " The servant of God, N., partakes of the precious and holy body and blood of our Lord and Saviour Jesus Christ to the remission of his sins and to eternal life " (See J. Goar, *Euchologion*, note 180, p. 153 : cf. p. 83, Paris edition 1647 ; F. E. Brightman, *Liturgies Eastern and Western*, i. 396).

But the mention of the body of the communicant in relation to the body of the Lord which is in the present English words of administration and which is made in connexion with Communion both by the Church of Rome and by the Eastern Church has a continuous history in Christian teaching.   A very remarkable instance of the importance attached to the bodily resurrection of Christ in its influence on Christian life is in St. Gregory of Nyssa, *Catechetical Oration* (about A.D. 385), 16.   Tertullian even in his Montanistic days emphasized the effect of the Sacraments as bringing the force of Christ's risen body into operation on Christian life by means of the bodily reception of them, and the value of this both for the present life and for the future resurrection.   See *e.g. On the resurrection of the flesh* (Africa, about A.D. 205), 8, " The flesh is washed that the soul may be cleansed ; the flesh is anointed that the soul may be hallowed ; the flesh is signed that the soul also may be strengthened ; the flesh is shadowed by the laying on of hands that the soul also may be enlightened by the Spirit ; the flesh feeds on the body and blood of Christ that the soul also may be nourished by God " ; *On chastity* (Africa, about A.D. 210), 16, " God both raised the Lord and will raise us through His own power because of the union of our body with the Lord."   Instances of teaching concerning the relation of Christians to the body of Christ through the administration of Baptism to their bodies are in St. Irenaeus, *Against Heresies* (Gaul, about A.D. 180), III. xvii. 2, and St. Leo, *Sermons*, lxiii. 6 (Rome, about A.D.

450), and through the reception of the Eucharist by their bodies in St. Irenaeus, *op. cit.* IV. xviii. 5 ; St. Cyril of Jerusalem, *Catechetical Lectures*, xxii. 3 (Jerusalem, about A.D. 348) ; St. Gregory of Nyssa, *op. cit.* 37 ; St. Leo, *Sermons*, lxiii. 7, *Epistles*, lix. 2.

NOTE 7. See p. 22

SACRIFICIAL INDICATIONS AT THE LAST SUPPER

For the sacrificial character of bread and wine among the Jews see *e.g.* Exod. xxix. 40 ; Lev. ii. xxiii. 13 ; Num. vi. 15, 17, xv. 5, 7, 10, xxviii. 14. Bread and wine were used in heathen sacrifices also, and so highly sacrificial words as " immolation " and " immolate " (*immolatio, immolo*) are derived from *mola* the meal which it was customary to strew on the victims at sacrifices. For the connexion of sacrifice with " covenant " see *e.g.* Exod. xxiv. 1–11. For the sacrificial use of " do " in a sacrificial context see *e.g.* Exod. xxix. 39. For the sacrificial use of " memorial " see *e.g.* Lev. xxiv. 7 ; Num. x. 10. For the sacrificial character of the pouring out of the blood see note 4 on p. 61 ; ἐκχυνόμενον is translated correctly " poured out " in the Revised Version of St. Luke xxii. 20 but incorrectly " shed " in St. Matt. xxvi. 28 and St. Mark xiv. 24. For the inconsistency of this see B. F. Westcott, *Some Lessons of the Revised Version of the New Testament*, p. 90, note.

NOTE 8. See p. 23

SACRIFICIAL TERMINOLOGY IN THE EARLY CHURCH

Instances of the terms mentioned in the sermon are *Teaching of the Twelve Apostles* (probably Syria, about A.D. 100), xiv. 1, 2 ; St. Ignatius (Antioch, about A.D. 110), *Ephesians*, 5, *Magnesians*, 7, *Trallians*, 7, *Philadelphians*, 4 (the connexion with the Eucharistic food, with the celebration of the Eucharist, and with the liturgical prayer of the Church, in *Ephesians*, 5, and *Philadelphians*, 4, is so close as to show that the Eucharist is in view) ; St. Justin Martyr, *Dialogue with Trypho*, 29, 41, 116, 117 ; St. Irenaeus (Gaul, about A.D. 180), *Against Heresies*, IV. xvii. 5, xviii. 1, 4 ; Tertullian, *On the crown*, 3, *Exhortation to chastity*, 11, *On single marriage*, 10, *On prayer*, 18, 19, *On Baptism*, 17, 19, *To Scapula*, 7 ; St. Cyprian (Africa, martyred A.D. 258), *On the unity of the Church*, 17, *On the lapsed*, 25, *Letters*, i. 2, xvi. 2, xvii. 2, lxiii. 9, 14. See further in the present writer's *A History of the Doctrine of the Holy Eucharist*, i. 46–54.

NOTE 9. See p. 27

The Eucharist regarded as a Spiritual Drama

For the conception of the Eucharist as a spiritual drama, see *e.g.* Nicolas Cabasilas, Metropolitan of Thessalonica in the middle of the fourteenth century, *Explanation of the Holy Liturgy*, especially cc. 1, 6, 8, 16, 37 ; Amalarius of Metz, Bishop of Treves A.D. 811, *On the Offices of the Church, Selections on the Office of the Mass* ; Ivo of Chartres, Bishop of Chartres A.D. 1091, *Sermons*, V ; W. Durand, Bishop of Mende, A.D. 1286, *Rationale of the Divine Offices*, IV. ; the book entitled *Ceremonies to be used in the Church of England together with an Explanation of the Meaning and Significancy of Them* drawn up about A.D. 1540 but not published at the time, printed early in the eighteenth century by the Nonjuror Jeremy Collier in his *An Ecclesiastical History cf Great Britain* ; see V. 110–117 for the section here referred to. See further on this subject the present writer's *A History of the Doctrine of the Holy Eucharist*, i. 168, 169, 210, 267–269, 272, ii. 120–124. Those who held this conception were prevented from regarding the Eucharist as merely a memory by their belief that the consecrated Sacrament really is the body and blood of Christ.

NOTE 10. See p. 28

IDEAS OF DESTRUCTION IN THE EUCHARISTIC SACRIFICE

The notion which underlies the theory that in sacrifice there must be destruction may be seen in the statement by St. Thomas Aquinas (died A.D. 1280), *Summa Theologica*, II², lxxxv. 3, " Sacrifices are properly so called when something is done in regard to things offered to God, as that animals were slain and burned, that bread is broken and eaten and blessed." Elaborate discussions on the subject are in the Latin divines of the sixteenth and seventeenth centuries. Theories minimizing or ignoring the element of destruction are those of Melchior Cano (Spanish Dominican, died A.D. 1560) that the sacrifice is in the consecration, the oblation of the consecrated Sacrament, the fraction of the consecrated host, and the consumption of the Sacrament (*De locis theologicis*, XII. xi. 69–74) ; of Alphonso Salmeron (Spanish Jesuit, died A.D. 1585) and Gabriel Vasquez (Spanish Jesuit, died A.D. 1604) that the crucial element in the sacrifice is in the mystically divided method of our Lord's sacramental existence under the two species (Salmeron, *Comment.* IX. xxix. ; Vasquez, *In S. T.* ccxxiii. 4) ; of Robert Bellarmine (Italian Jesuit, died A.D. 1621) that the sacrifice consists in the consecration and communion taken together (*De Missa*, i. 2, 27) ; and of Francis Suarez (Spanish Jesuit, died A.D. 1617) that the sacrifice consists in the presence of the body and blood of Christ on the altar as an offering in honour of God (*Disp.* lxxiii. 6 (3), lxxv. 2–5). On the other hand, a famous instance of emphasizing the element of destruction is in John de

Lugo (Spanish Jesuit, died A.D. 1660) who taught that by consecration the body of Christ is brought into a lower state so as to be fit for food and drink and in the condition of a victim (*De Euch.* xix. iv. v. 67). For a fuller discussion of this subject see *A History of the Doctrine of the Holy Eucharist*, ii. 356–377, 387–397.

NOTE 11. See p. 28

THE EUCHARISTIC SACRIFICE AND OUR LORD'S LIFE IN HEAVEN

The connexion of the Eucharist with our Lord's risen and heavenly life was suggested by writers of the early Church, as *e.g.* St. Ignatius, *Smyrn.* 6; St. Irenaeus, *Against Heresies*, IV. xviii. 6; Origen (Alexandria, died A.D. 253), *In Leu. Hom.* vi. 2, vii. 2, ix. 1, 3, 4, 5, 6, 9, 10, *In Jud. Hom.* vii. 2, *Mart.* 30, 39, *In Jer. Hom.* xviii. 13 (al. xix.); St. Gregory of Nazianzus (died A.D 392). *Orat.* xxvi. 16, xlv. 23–25; St. Chrysostom (Antioch and Constantinople, died A.D. 407), *In Heb. Hom.* xi. 2, 3, xiv. 1, 2, *De Sac.* iii. 4; St. Ambrose (Milan, died A.D. 397), *In Ps.* xxxviii. *Enar.* 25, *De off.* i. 248, *De fid.* iii. 87; the author of *De Sacramentis* (North Italy, about A.D. 400) iv. 27; St. Augustine (Africa, died A.D. 430), *In Ps.* xxv. *Enar.* ii. 10, *In Ps.* lxiv. *Enar.* 6, *Serm.* cccli. 7. In the middle ages reference was made to it by Eastern writers, *e.g.* Oecumenius (Thessaly, latter half of century x.), On Heb. viii. 1–6, xiii. 9–11; Theophylact (Bulgaria, died A.D. 1107), On Heb. vii. 25, viii. 3, ix. 24; Euthymius Zigabenus (Constantinople, died about A.D. 1118), On Heb. vii. 25, viii. 2, 4, 6, ix. 24, 25, x. 11, 12, xiii. 9. In more recent times it was strongly emphasized by the French writers Charles de Condren (died A.D. 1641) in his *The Idea of the Priesthood and Sacrifice of Jesus Christ*, John James Olier (died 1657) in his *Explanation of the Ceremonies of the Parochial High Mass*, and Louis Thomassin (died 1696) in the section *On the Incarnation of the Word of God* of his *Theological Dogmas* (X. vi.—xiv., xvii.—xix., xxix., xxxi). See the *A History of the Doctrine of the Holy Eucharist*, i. 50–52, 116–121, 156–161, ii. 377–387, 586–603.

F

NOTE **12.**   See p. 34

The Greek Mysteries

There is an illuminating account of the Greek mysteries in E. Hatch, *The influence of Greek Ideas and Usages upon the Christian Church*, pp. 283–292. See also F. B. Jevons, *An Introduction to the History of Religion*, pp. 327–381 ; F. Cumont, *Les religions orientales dans le paganisme romain ;* K. Lake, *The Earlier Epistles of St. Paul*, pp. 40–47, 196–198, 216, 217 ; H. A. A. Kennedy, *St. Paul and the Mystery Religions ;* A. Loisy, *Les mystères païens et le mystère Chrétien.* The influence of the mysteries on Christianity probably has been greatly exaggerated by some writers.

NOTE **13.** See p. 40

CALVIN'S THEORY OF SACRIFICE IN THE EUCHARIST

For this theory see *e.g.* J. Calvin, *Institutes of the Christian Religion* (A.D. 1559), IV. xviii. ; T. Cranmer, *A Defence of the True and Catholic Doctrine of the Sacrament of the Body and Blood of our Saviour Christ* (A.D. 1551), and *An Answer unto a Crafty and Sophistical Cavillation devised by Stephen Gardiner* (A.D. 1551) ; J. Jewel, *A Reply unto M. Harding's Answer* (A.D. 1562). See further vol. ii. of *A History of the Doctrine of the Holy Eucharist.*

NOTE 14. See p. 42

ZWINGLI'S EUCHARISTIC TEACHING

For the illustrations used by Zwingli mentioned in the sermon see his *Clear Explanation of the Lord's Supper* (A.D. 1526) (*Opera*, ed. 1581, ii. 293) and a sermon preached at Berne in A.D. 1528 (ii. 532). For a fuller treatment of his teaching see *A History of the Doctrine of the Holy Eucharist*, ii. 37–43.

NOTE **15.** See p. 43

VIRTUALISM

For Virtualism see *e.g.* T. Cranmer, *A Defence of the True and Catholic Doctrine of the Sacrament of the Body and Blood of our Saviour Christ,* and *An Answer unto a Crafty and Sophistical Cavillation devised by Stephen Gardiner.* See further vol. ii. of *A History of the Doctrine of the Holy Eucharist.*

NOTE **16.** See p. 43

RECEPTIONISM

For Receptionism see *e.g.* M. Bucer, *Nine Propositions concerning the Holy Eucharist* (A.D. 1530) (in *Martini Buceri Scripta Anglicana*, p. 611) ; J. Calvin, *Institutes of the Christian Religion*, IV. xvii. ; J. Cosin, *A Paper Concerning the Differences in the Chief Points of Religion betwixt the Church of Rome and the Church of England* (published A.D. 1705 ; Cosin died A.D. 1672) (*Works* in *Anglo-Catholic Library*, iv. 336), and *Historia Transubstantiationis Papalis* (published A.D. 1675) (*Works*, iv. 16–19, 46–49) ; J. Taylor, *Real Presence and Spiritual* (A.D. 1654) and *Dissuasive from Popery* (A.D. 1664). See further vol. ii. of *A History of the Doctrine of the Holy Eucharist*.

NOTE 17. See p. 45

THE AGENT IN CONSECRATION

For the ordinary Western teaching that in the consecration the priest speaks in the Person of Christ see *e.g.* St. Thomas Aquinas, *Summa Theologica* (died A.D. 1274), III. lxxviii. 1, " The form of this Sacrament is pronounced as if in the person of Christ Himself speaking so that we may be able to understand that the minister in the performance of this Sacrament does nothing except pronounce the words of Christ." Compare III. lxxxii. 1, 2 ad 2, 3, 7 ad 3, where it is said that the priest consecrates " in the person of Christ," III. lxxxiii. 1 ad 3, " the priest bears the image of Christ, in whose person and power he utters the words of consecration," and III. lxii. 1, where God is called the " causa agens principalis " (" principal acting cause ") and the " principalis agens " (" principal agent ") in the Sacraments. In III. lxxx. 12 ad 3 St. Thomas says that " the priest in the person of all offers and receives the blood," and in III. lxxxii. 7 ad 3 that "In the Mass the priest speaks in the prayers in the person of the Church in the unity of which he has his place, but in the consecration of the Sacrament he speaks in the person of Christ whose office he holds through the power of Order." For Western teaching that the priest offers in the person of the whole Church see *e.g.* Duns Scotus (died A.D. 1308), *Quaestiones Quodlibetales*, xx, " The Mass . . . avails not only by virtue of the personal merit of the priest who offers but also by virtue of the general merit of the Church, in the person of which the sacrifice is offered by means of the minister of all.") For the Eastern theory of consecration see Note **18.** on p. 80.

NOTE 18. See p. 45

THE MOMENT OF CONSECRATION

The Church of England very explicitly accepts the Western theory that the consecration is effected by the recital of the words of institution.   This is shown by the provision in the Book of Common Prayer, " If the consecrated Bread or Wine be all spent before all have communicated, the Priest is to consecrate more according to the form before prescribed : beginning at ' Our Saviour Christ in the same night etc.' for the blessing of the Bread ; and at ' Likewise after Supper etc.' for the blessing of the Cup."   In the Roman Missal the priest is directed to adore after the recital of the words of institution in the case of each species, and there is a provision (*De defectibus*, x. 13) that in the event of an accident to the chalice the priest is to consecrate by reciting the words of institution ; " If none at all is left, he is again to place wine and water [in the chalice] and to consecrate from the place ' Likewise after supper,' having first made an oblation of the chalice."   For the Eastern theory of consecration see *e.g.* St. John of Damascus (died about A.D. 765), *On the Orthodox Faith*, iv. 13, " The bread that is offered and the wine and water are by means of the invocation and descent of the Holy Ghost supernaturally transmade into the body and the blood of Christ " ; *The Orthodox Confession of the Catholic and Apostolic Eastern Church* (A.D. 1640), i. 107, " The priest must know that at the moment when he consecrates the gifts the substance itself of the bread and the substance of the wine are changed into the substance of the real body and blood of Christ by means of the

operation of the Holy Ghost whom he invokes at that
time, consecrating this mystery by praying and saying
' Send down Thy Holy Ghost on us and on these gifts
set before Thee, and make this bread the precious body
of Thy Christ and that which is in this cup the precious
blood of Thy Christ, changing them by Thy Holy Ghost,'
For immediately after these words the Transubstantiation takes place, and the bread is changed into the real
body of Christ, and the wine into His real blood."

NOTE **19.** See p. 46

THE EARLY CHURCH AND TRANSUBSTANTIATION

For the tendency in the fourth and fifth centuries towards Transubstantiation see St. Gregory of Nyssa (died about A.D. 395), *Catechetical Oration*, 37 ; St. Chrysostom, *Homilies on St. Matthew*, lxxxii. 5, *Homilies on I Corinthians*, xxiv. 2 ; St. Cyril of Alexandria (died A.D. 444), *Commentary on St. Luke*, on xxii. 19, 20 ; compare St. Cyril of Jerusalem, *Catechetical Lectures*, xxii. 2, 3, 9, 20 ; St. Ambrose, *On faith*, iv. 124. For the tendency in the other direction see Nestorius (Constantinople, died about A.D. 450), *Bazaar of Heraclides*, in J. F. Bethune-Baker, *Nestorius and his Teaching*, pp. 145, 146, and F. Nau, *Le livre d'Héraclide de Damas*, p. 288 ; Theodoret (Syria, died about A.D. 457), *Dialogues*, ii. ; Pope Gelasius (Rome, died A.D. 496), *On the two natures in Christ*, in A. Thiel, *Epistolae Romanorum Pontificum Genuinae*, i. 541, 542. See further *A History of the Doctrine of the Holy Eucharist*, i. 98–106.

NOTE **20.** See p. 52

THE COUNCIL OF NICAEA (A.D. 325) AND THE DYING

Canon 13, " Concerning those who are at the point of death the ancient and canonical law shall still be observed so that if any is departing he shall not be deprived of the last and most necessary Viaticum. But, if after having been despaired of (ἀπογνωσθείς) and re-admitted to Communion he is again found among the living, let him take his place with those who have fellowship in prayer only. But generally also in the case of every person whatsoever departing this life who asks to receive the Eucharist let the bishop test his fitness and administer it."

NOTE 21. See p. 55

The Appeal of the Early Apologists to Christian Morality

See *e.g.* the *Apology* of Aristides, 15, 16 (Syriac text), "The Christians . . . do not commit adultery nor fornication, they do not bear false witness, they do not deny a deposit nor covet what is not theirs ; they honour father and mother ; they do good to those who are their neighbours, and when they are judges they judge uprightly ; . . . whatever they do not wish that others should do to them, they do not practise towards any one ; . . . their wives, O king, are pure as virgins, and their daughters modest : and their men abstain from all unlawful wedlock and from all impurity ; . . . they walk in all humility and kindness, and falsehood is not found among them, and they love one another. . . . As men who know God, they ask from Him petitions which are proper for Him to give and for them to receive : and thus they accomplish the course of their lives. And because they acknowledge the goodnesses of God towards them, lo ! on account of them there flows forth the beauty that is in the world. . . . And I have no doubt that the world stands by reason of the intercession of Christians " (translation in *Texts and Studies*, I. i. 48–51) ; *Epistle to Diognetus*, 5, 6, " Christians . . . spend time on earth but their citizenship is in heaven. They obey the established laws and they surpass the laws in their own lives. They love all and are persecuted by all. They are ignored and yet they are condemned. They are put to death and yet they are filled with life. They are poor and yet they make many rich. They lack all things and yet abound in all things. . . . They are reviled and yet they bless. They are insulted and yet they respect. Doing good they are punished as if evil. Being punished they rejoice as if filled with life. . . . What the soul is in a body, this Christians are in the world "; St. Justin Martyr, *First Apology*, 14, " We who formerly delighted in fornication now strive only for purity ; . . . we who loved the paths to riches and possessions above everything else now make what we have common and share it with every one who is in need ; we who hated and killed one another . . . now since the coming of Christ live together and pray for our enemies and try to persuade those who hate us unjustly so that they who have lived in accordance with the fair precepts of Christ may have good hope of obtaining the same reward as ourselves from God the Ruler of all."

NOTE 22. See p. 56

THE PHRASE CHRIST-BEARER

Christians are called " Christ-bearers " by St. Ignatius about A.D. 110 in his *Epistle to the Ephesians*, 9, " So then ye are all companions in the way, God-bearers and shrine-bearers, Christ-bearers (χριστοφόροι), bearers of holy things, arrayed throughout in the commandments of Jesus Christ "). " Christ-bearer " is used as an epithet of the martyrs by Phileas (of Thmuis in Egypt, martyred A.D. 306) quoted by Eusebius, *Church History*, VIII. x. 3 ; of St. Paul by Adamantius (probably Antioch about A.D. 335), *Dialogue*, v. 22, and by St. Athanasius (Alexandria, died A.D. 373), *Against the heathen*, 5, *On the Incarnation*, 10 ; of orthodox Christians by St. Athanasius, *Orations against the Arians*, iii. 45. St. Cyril of Jerusalem (preaching c. A.D. 348, died A.D. 386) calls the water in Baptism " Christ-bearing," *Procatechesis*, 15, " Then may ye enjoy the Christ-bearing waters that have fragrance," and describes Christians as becoming " Christ-bearers " at the reception of the Eucharist, *Catechetical Lectures*, xxii. 3, " With all assurance let us partake as of the body and blood of Christ. For in the figure of bread is given to thee His body, and in the figure of wine is given to thee His blood, that by partaking of the body and blood of Christ thou mayest be made of one body and blood with Him. For thus indeed we become Christ-bearers when His body and blood are imparted to our members. For so it is that according to the blessed Peter [2 St. Peter i. 4] we become partakers of the divine nature."

INDEX OF QUOTATIONS